NADIYA'S

Bake Me a Story

NADIYA'S

Bake Me a Story

Nadiya Hussain

illustrated by Clair Rossiter

Hodder
Children's
Books

HODDER CHILDREN'S BOOKS

First published in Great Britain in 2016 by Hodder and Stoughton

3 5 7 9 10 8 6 4 2

A CIP catalogue record for this book
is available from the British Library.

ISBN 978 1 444 93327 7

Edited by Emma Goldhawk
Designed by Alison Padley

Photography by Dan Annett
Food styling by Shokofeh Hejazi
Food photography by Joe Woodhouse

Repro at Born Group
Printed and bound in Germany by Mohn Media

The paper and board used in this book
are made from wood from responsible sources

MIX
Paper from
responsible sources
FSC® C104740

Hodder Children's Books
An imprint of
Hachette Children's Group
Part of Hodder and Stoughton
Carmelite House
50 Victoria Embankment
London EC4Y 0DZ

An Hachette UK Company
www.hachette.co.uk

www.hachettechildrens.co.uk

To my three beautiful children,
Musa, Dawud and Maryam.
Your love of reading and being read to while I've
been elbow-deep in the kitchen inspired this book.
"Why can't we read and cook at the same time?"
they asked. The rest, as they say, is history.

Hello!

I'm Nadiya, and these are my three kids, Musa, Dawud and Maryam. It's lovely to meet you!

There are two special things that my family and I love to do together — baking and sharing stories. I wrote *Bake Me a Story* to bring both of those special things together in one book so you can enjoy them too.

As you will discover inside, each chapter has a story and a recipe. You could read the story first and then make the recipe, or you could enjoy reading while your bake is in the oven.

While you are waiting for your pumpkin flapjacks to go golden brown in the oven, why not curl up with the story of 'Cinderella, the Party and the Pumpkins'? Or meet Little Red Hen, who loves baking bread, before making a delicious blueberry and orange soda loaf of your own. It doesn't matter which way round you enjoy the baking and the stories — all that matters is that you have fun!

There are useful tips from me on the next page, as well as with every recipe. Grown-ups, you might find some of the tips on the recipe pages helpful if you are baking with kids of different ages.

So, pop on your apron and wash your hands – it's time
to get busy as we bake and share stories.

Meet you in the kitchen!

Love,

Nadiya

Dawud

Maryam

Musa

x x x x

HELPFUL HINTS AND TASTY TIPS

Safety in the kitchen

Always make sure a grown-up is with you in the kitchen.

Don't touch the kitchen knives – they are sharp! If a grown-up says you can use them to chop or slice, be very careful.

Ask a grown-up to help you if you are using a food processor.

Always wash your hands in warm soapy water before you start.

Be careful of the hot oven and hobs.

Oven temperature

All the recipes in this book have been tested in a fan-assisted oven. If you are using a conventional oven, increase the temperature by 20°C.

Measurements

g – grams
ml – millilitres
tsp – teaspoon
tbsp – tablespoon
°C – degrees celsius

Recipe guide

Every recipe has a guide to show you how easy or difficult it might be. Always make sure a grown-up is with you when you try any of these recipes, especially when it needs a knife or a food processor, or involves anything hot.

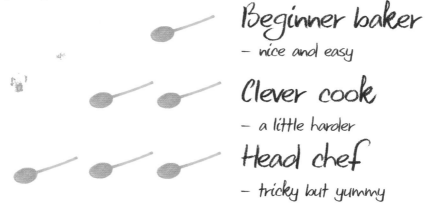

Beginner baker
– nice and easy

Clever cook
– a little harder

Head chef
– tricky but yummy

CONTENTS

The Not-Just-Ginger
GINGERBREAD GUY

It was nearly elevenses time, and a little
old lady was at home with nothing to dunk in her cup of tea. She
rootled through her cupboards. There were no chocolate cookies,
no figgy rolls – not even any plain old crackers. But she could see
lots of flour, brown sugar, honey and jars upon jars of spices.

The little old lady decided to make her favourite biscuit – a
gingerbread guy. But when she went to add her ginger, she realised
that there wasn't quite enough left in the jar for her recipe. So the
old lady reached for another of the spice jars instead. The label
read 'star anise'. She gave the jar a sniff – it smelled sweet and
smoky and a little bit magical, so the little old lady measured out
a tablespoon of star anise, added it to the mixture, and put her
gingerbread guy in the oven to cook.

After fifteen minutes, the cottage was filled with the most
delicious smells. The old lady took the gingerbread guy out of the
oven and turned to put the kettle on. But when she turned back,
she couldn't believe her eyes – the gingerbread guy had jumped
off the baking tray and was running out of the front door.

"Don't go, gingerbread guy!" cried the little old lady. "I want to dunk you in my tea!"

She kicked off her carpet slippers and chased her biscuit down the street. When she caught up with the gingerbread guy, the old lady grabbed his little arm but he was still too hot from the oven. "Ow!" she cried, and let him go.

The gingerbread guy ran on down the street. Before long he came to a field, where he ran past a cow.

"Stop, little gingerbread guy!" mooed the cow. "I'm fed up of eating grass. I'd love a biscuit instead."

The gingerbread guy didn't stop, so the cow gave chase. When she caught up with the gingerbread guy, she gave him a big sniff.

"You smell different . . ." the cow said, confused. And while the cow was having a good long think, the gingerbread guy sneaked away.

He ran on until he came to a river.

"If my feet get wet, they will fall off," the gingerbread guy said to himself. "How am I going to get across?"

"Allow me to help, young biscuit," said a fox, appearing from behind a bush. "Jump up on to my tail and I will carry you across the river. You can trust me. Foxes don't eat gingerbread."

The gingerbread guy didn't know that really, foxes absolutely LOVE gingerbread, so he jumped on to the fox's tail and the fox plunged into the river.

"My feet are getting wet!" said the gingerbread guy.

"You're too heavy for my tail," said the fox. "Jump up onto my back."

So the gingerbread guy jumped onto the fox's furry back. But before long, the fox's back started to get wet too.

"You're too heavy for my back," said the fox. "You'll have to jump up on to my head."

So the gingerbread guy jumped on to the fox's head. But it wasn't long before the water was rising again.

The gingerbread guy was so worried about his feet. If they got soggy and fell off, he wouldn't be able to carry on running when he got to the other side.

"There's only one way to keep your feet dry," said the fox. "You'll have to keep jumping high in the air, until we reach the riverbank."

So the gingerbread man jumped as high as he could.

The sly fox tipped his head back, his jaws wide open.

The gingerbread guy landed in the fox's mouth, and … *SNAP!* the fox's jaws closed shut.

"*Pah!*" The fox spat out the gingerbread guy in surprise. "*You taste different!*" he spluttered.

Then the fox realised his mistake. "*But, different tastes sooooooo good! Come back, so I can eat you properly!*"

The not-just-ginger gingerbread guy laughed. "*That'll be the star anise!*" he yelled over his shoulder to the fox. And on his little dry feet, he carried on running.

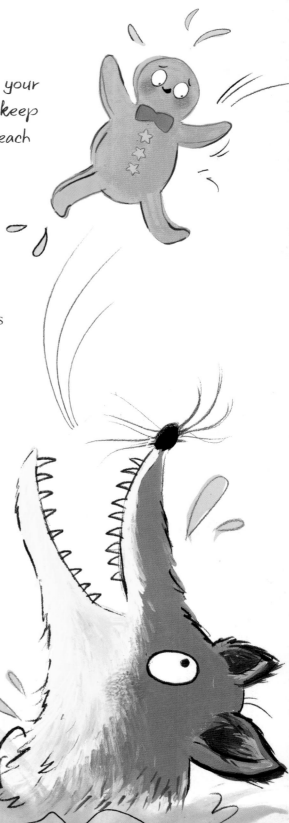

STAR ANISE GINGERBREAD MEN

Makes about 30

Ingredients

175g golden caster sugar

6 tbsp clear runny honey

1 tbsp orange juice

1 tsp vanilla extract

2 tbsp ground ginger

1 tbsp ground star anise

(You will need a spice grinder for the star anise, or you can swap it for the same quantity of ground nutmeg)

200g unsalted butter

450g plain flour, sifted, plus extra for dusting

1 tsp bicarbonate of soda

¼ tsp salt

writing icing tubes, for decoration

Method

- ✿ Place the caster sugar, honey, orange juice, vanilla extract, ginger and star anise in a pan over a medium heat and stir until all the sugar has dissolved.

- ✿ Remove from the heat and add the butter. Stir until it has melted, then set aside and leave to cool.

- ✿ Once cool, add the flour, bicarbonate of soda and salt, and bring the dough together. Wrap the dough in cling film and chill for at least 2 hours.

- ✿ Line two baking sheets with greaseproof paper.

- ✿ Remove the dough from the fridge, unwrap it and roll it out on a lightly floured surface to a thickness of about 0.5cm. Cut out shapes with a gingerbread-man cutter – a 7.5cm cutter will make around 30 biscuits.

- ✿ Gather off-cuts and re-roll the dough as necessary.

- ✿ Place the gingerbread men on the lined baking sheets and transfer to the freezer for 10 minutes to firm up. Preheat the oven to 180°C fan/gas mark 6.

- ✿ Transfer the sheets from the freezer to the oven and bake for 15 minutes, or until golden around the edges and paler in the centre.

- ✿ Remove from the oven and leave to cool on the sheets for 10 minutes, then transfer to a wire rack.

- ✿ Have fun decorating your gingerbread men with icing!

Nadiya's tip
You could try raisins for eyes, or chocolate drops for buttons. Attach them to the gingerbread with writing icing.

Ruby-Red, the Three Bears and the
VERY-BERRY BREAKFAST

Once upon a very long time ago, there

were three bears who really loved to eat breakfast. And for their breakfast, they really, REALLY loved to eat porridge.

Dad Bear had got up bright and early one morning to make the porridge, but there was nothing in the cupboard to use as a topping. And all bears know that porridge is always best with something tasty on top …

"I know," said Mum Bear. "We could go into the forest and see what kind of fruit we can find."

Little Bear's favourite porridge topping was berries, and Mum knew just where to find the bushes to pick them, so the three bears put on their coats and boots and headed into the forest.

Meanwhile, Ruby-Red, a little girl from the village, was out shopping for some baking ingredients. She had bought flour, oats, brown sugar, bananas, eggs, oil and milk, but she still needed berries.

"Ooh! I know where I can find the tastiest, juiciest berries," said Ruby-Red, and she skipped off in the direction of the forest. But when Ruby-Red got to the bears' cottage, she stopped and thought for a second.

"All this skipping has tired me out. And my shopping is very heavy," Ruby-Red said to herself. "I could have a little nap before I go and find my berries ..."

And so, Ruby-Red crept inside.

She went into the kitchen and spotted three bowls of porridge on the table.

"Well," said Ruby-Red. "I am also a bit hungry. Before I have my nap and before I find my berries, I could eat a little something ..."

The first bowl of porridge was too hot. Ruby-Red burned her tongue. The second bowl of porridge was too cold. Ruby-Red didn't like cold porridge.

But the third bowl of porridge was just right. So Ruby-Red ate the lot.

Then she climbed the stairs, curled up in a bed and fell fast asleep.

The bears returned home with basketfuls of juicy berries. But they soon noticed something was different in their kitchen.

"Someone's had a spoonful of my porridge!" said Dad Bear.

"Someone's had a spoonful of my porridge!" said Mum Bear.

"Someone's eaten ALL of my porridge!" said Little Bear, and burst into tears.

Ruby-Red woke up at the sound. She was sorry that she'd made Little Bear cry.

"Erm, hello, big scary bears," Ruby-Red said, coming into the kitchen and giving the three bears a fright. "I ate your breakfast. Sorry about that. Please don't eat me instead."

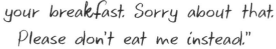

Then she spotted the pile of berries sitting on the table, and a plan popped into Ruby-Red's head.

"How would you like me to make you something different for your breakfast today?" she asked, and opened her shopping bag. "I have everything I need for a tasty treat, apart from berries."

"Well, I think we can help you there ..." said Mum Bear.

So Ruby-Red handed Little Bear a wooden spoon, and they baked a batch of delicious very-berry breakfast muffins together.

VERY-BERRY
BREAKFAST MUFFINS

Makes 12

Ingredients

200g plain flour

200g rolled porridge oats

75g soft light brown sugar

3 tsp baking powder

Pinch of salt

2 large eggs

2 ripe bananas, mashed

3 tbsp sunflower oil

250ml whole milk

50g blueberries

75g raspberries, halved

Nadiya's tip

You can swap fresh berries for raisins.
Give the raisins a light coating of flour
first to stop them sinking to the bottom.

Method

Preheat the oven to 200°C fan/gas mark 7. Line a 12-hole muffin tin with muffin cases.

Combine the flour, oats, sugar, baking powder and salt in a bowl.

Mix the eggs with the mashed bananas in a separate bowl then add the wet mixture to the dry ingredients.

Add the sunflower oil and milk, and give it all a good mix, then add the berries and mix again.

Half-fill each muffin case with the mixture then place the tin in the oven and bake for 25 minutes, or until the muffins are well-risen and golden on top.

Remove from the oven and leave to cool for 5 minutes, then enjoy them warm!

18

Jack and the BEAN-PATTY STALK

Jack, a very small lad with a very big heart, lived on a very small farm with his very small mother. They had a very small field, on which they kept a very small sheep called Minnie. Everything was very small, but Jack and his mother didn't mind – it was theirs, and that's what mattered.

But, one winter, bad weather ruined all their crops and the food in their very small cupboard ran out. There were not even beans to make Jack's favourite patties. Jack and his mother dearly loved Minnie the sheep but they knew it was time to sell her.

"We need money to buy food, Jack, but we have nothing to sell except our dear little sheep," Jack's mother said, a tear in her eye. "You must take Minnie to market. Be sure to get a good price for her. Her wool is the softest in the land."

So Jack led Minnie the very small sheep away from the very small farm. But because Jack was so hungry, he had already forgotten what his mother had told him to do.

He came across a man on the road to market.

"That is the most beautiful little sheep I have ever seen," the man told Jack. "I will give you five magic butter beans for her."

"Why are they magic?" Jack asked.

"They are the finest beans in the land and they will yield a crop like no other," the man replied.

"That sounds like a fair deal," Jack said. "Minnie's wool is the finest in the land too." Poor Jack had an empty tummy and an empty head.

So off Jack went with his butter beans. He had a spring in his step and a song in his very big heart. But when he got back to his mother, she yelled at him in a surprisingly loud voice for a very small lady.

"You sold our sheep for FIVE BUTTER BEANS?" she yelled. "We can't even grow crops on our land, Jack! These beans are worthless to us!"

Jack's mother threw the beans out of the window and stormed upstairs to bed.

Jack felt awful. He wasn't quite sure what to do, so he just curled up in his very small armchair and went to sleep.

The next morning, Jack woke up to a weird rustling sound. He looked out of

the window but all he could see was a forest of bright green leaves. Fighting his way out of the front door, he looked up and gasped. An enormous beanstalk had appeared from nowhere, stretching all the way up to the sky.

A giant beanstalk means giant beans! Jack thought to himself. *Maybe we'll have something to eat, after all.*

So Jack started to climb. It took a while but eventually he poked his head through the clouds at the top of the beanstalk.

Jack couldn't believe his eyes. There in front of him were piles and piles and piles of butter beans, and sat among them all was a huge, hairy giant! There was a thunderous rumbling sound, and the giant rubbed his tummy.

"Fee ... fie ... fuddly ... foo ... Oh, why can't I remember the words?" the giant wailed. "Fee ... fie ... flopsie ... flip ... That's not it, either!"

A tear the size of a fishpond rolled down the giant's nose and splashed on to the ground, nearly drowning Jack.

"Er ... excuse me, very large giant man?" Jack squeaked. "I ... um ... heard your tummy rumbling just now. I think you are forgetting things because you are hungry."

The giant squinted at the ground. "I AM hungry, very small person," said the giant. "I am too big to go to market, so all I have eaten for years and years is butter beans. I just can't bear to eat another one ever again."

"Well, Mr Giant, I'm hungry too," said Jack. "If you give me some gold, maybe we can help each other out."

So the giant gave Jack a golden coin that was almost as tall as he was. Jack scrambled back down the beanstalk with it and ran all the way to market without stopping.

Jack spent the gold on crates of eggs and sacks of breadcrumbs, herbs and spices. He called his mother, told her his plan, and they hauled the crates and sacks up the beanstalk together.

"*Dinner's ready!*" Jack announced after a short while. He and his mother dropped a huge stack of steaming butter-bean patties in front of the giant.

The giant declared the patties to be the yummiest food he had ever tasted, and invited Jack and his mother to tuck in too.

"*FEE ... FIE ... FO ... FUM!*" the giant roared in delight once his tummy was full and his memory had returned. "*From now on,*" he declared, "*I will give you gold to buy ingredients, if you will make me tasty meals from my beans. You will always be welcome to eat here with me, any time you like.*"

And Jack and his mother never went hungry again.

25

JACK'S BEAN PATTIES

Makes 12

Ingredients

2 x 400g can butter beans, drained and rinsed

100g breadcrumbs

½ tsp paprika

1 tsp cumin powder

1 tsp mild curry powder

Handful of coriander, leaves and stems, roughly chopped

1 tsp salt

2 eggs

Nadiya's tip

Don't forget to give your hands a good wash with soapy water before you start!

Method

- Preheat the oven to 180C fan. Line a baking tray with greaseproof paper.
- Tip the beans into a bowl and crush with a potato masher. Add the breadcrumbs, spices, salt, coriander and eggs.
- Using damp hands, mix everything together and make six bean patties.
- Bake for 25-30 minutes, until golden brown and crisp around the edges.
- You can eat in baps as a burger or with a salad.

Little Red Hen and her
BREAD FRIENDS

Little Red Hen was best friends with

Big Brown Dog, Sleek Ginger Cat and Squeaky Black Rat. One sunny morning, Little Red Hen decided she would like to do some baking.

"Will you come with me to buy the flour?" Little Red Hen asked Big Brown Dog.

"Not right now, Little Red Hen. I'm a little busy," said Big Brown Dog, and rushed away.

"That's a shame. I will go and buy it myself," said Little Red Hen.

"Will you help me find some baking powder?" Little Red Hen asked Squeaky Black Rat.

"Sorry! Got too much to do," said Squeaky Black Rat, and scuttled out of sight.

"OK, I will find it myself," said Little Red Hen.

"Will you help me get water from the well?" Little Red Hen asked Sleek Ginger Cat.

"Apologies. Now's not a good time," said Sleek Ginger Cat, and disappeared from view.

"I suppose I will get it by myself, then," said Little Red Hen. She was really confused. It wasn't like her friends to be unhelpful.

"Will you help me make the bread?" Little Red Hen asked them all a little later.

"Sorry, can't help," said Rat, Cat and Dog. And they all scampered off together.

"I shall make the bread all by myself," said Little Red Hen. "And then eat it all by myself, too," she added, grumpily.

Little Red Hen popped on her apron, lit the oven, washed her feathers and got to work. She was still a bit upset, so she gave the mixture a very enthusiastic stir.

Then Rat, Cat and Dog peeked around the kitchen door.

Little Red Hen pretended not to notice them.

"How's the bread looking, Hen?" they asked.

Little Red Hen pretended not to hear them.

Then the trio shuffled into the kitchen and presented Little Red Hen with a basket that was overflowing with fruit.

"SURPRISE!" shouted Rat, Cat and Dog. "We wanted to find you the yummiest blueberries and the juiciest oranges for your bread."

Little Red Hen was filled with joy. Her friends had done something lovely for her.

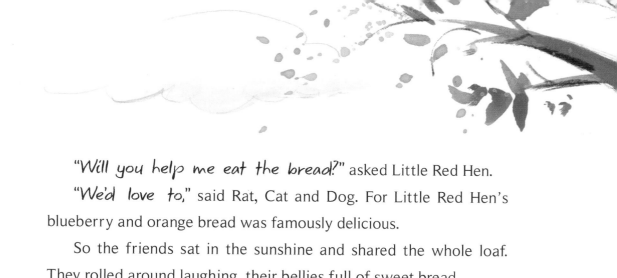

"Will you help me eat the bread?" asked Little Red Hen.

"We'd love to," said Rat, Cat and Dog. For Little Red Hen's blueberry and orange bread was famously delicious.

So the friends sat in the sunshine and shared the whole loaf. They rolled around laughing, their bellies full of sweet bread.

"What's better than best friends?" Little Red Hen asked Rat, Cat and Dog. "Bread friends, of course!"

BLUEBERRY AND ORANGE SODA BREAD

Makes one loaf

Ingredients

400g plain flour

2 tsp baking powder

½ tsp salt

50g caster sugar

2 tbsp light olive oil

100g dried blueberries

grated zest of 2 oranges

1 large egg

185ml buttermilk

Nadiya's tip

If baking with more than one child, the younger child could stir the mixture and the older child shape the dough into a ball.

Method

- Preheat the oven to 180°C fan/gas mark 6. Line a baking tray with greaseproof paper.

- Sift the flour into a bowl, then add the baking powder, salt, sugar, olive oil, blueberries and orange zest and stir to combine.

- Beat the egg with the buttermilk in a jug.

- Mix the wet ingredients into the dry ingredients with a spatula, then gently bring the dough together by hand, to form a ball. Don't overwork it!

- Place the dough on the lined tray and make two deep cuts on the top in a cross shape, nearly all the way through. Bake for 30–35 minutes, or until the loaf sounds hollow when tapped on the base.

- Remove from the oven and transfer to a wire rack to cool.

The Never-ending
PORRIDGE PAN

A little boy

sat cross-legged under a tree in the park, looking really sad. He was hungry, and his tummy was rumbling like thunder.

An elderly woman walked by pulling her shopping trolley behind her.

"What on earth is that rumbling sound?" the old woman said.

"It's my tummy," said the little boy. "I haven't had any breakfast and I am really, REALLY hungry."

The old woman gave the little boy a wink and started rummaging in her trolley. She pulled out an old bashed-up saucepan and handed it to him.

"With this, you'll never be hungry again," said the old woman.

The little boy peered into the saucepan, but it was empty. He stuck his hand in, then he tipped it upside down, just in case he'd missed something, but there was definitely nothing to eat inside. The boy was about to hand the pan back to the old woman when she got a wooden spoon out of her trolley and tapped it on the pan's rim.

"Cook, little pan, cook," she said. And to the boy's delight, the saucepan suddenly filled up with warm, creamy porridge!

"Stop, little pan, stop," said the old woman. The saucepan stopped filling.

The little boy grabbed the wooden spoon and began shovelling porridge into his mouth.

"THNKKYOOVRYMCCHH," he said, his mouth full.

"The pot is yours now," the old woman replied. "But remember, you must always tap the pot as you say the magic words." And with that, she picked up her shopping trolley and trundled away.

The little boy rushed home to show the saucepan to his dad. They couldn't believe their luck. The boy showed his dad what the old woman had taught him.

"Cook, little pan, cook," Dad said as he tapped the pan. His eyes popped out on stalks when he saw the porridge magically appearing.

"*Stop, little pan, stop,*" said Dad. He tried stopping and starting a few more times, just for the fun of it.

It was just as the old woman promised – the little boy and his dad would always have food now, whenever they needed it.

One morning, Dad came back from a night shift and tapped the magic pan, asking it to cook him some porridge. Then he slumped on the sofa … and promptly fell asleep. When the little boy got home from school that afternoon, he realised something was wrong.

There was a smell of warm milk wafting through the letterbox, and the front door wouldn't open.

The boy shoved hard at the door, and as it finally gave way, with a *WHOOOSSSHHHH*, he was knocked off his feet by a wave of gloopy, sticky porridge!

The little boy wiped the gloop from his eyes and watched in amazement as Dad sailed out of the front door on the wave of porridge, still asleep on the sofa.

"*STOP, LITTLE PAN, STOP!*" the boy yelled, but it was no good – the porridge continued to gush from his house. He needed to tap the saucepan as he said the magic words.

There was only one thing for it. He stuck his face into the porridge and started to eat.

Two hours later, the boy had eaten his way through the front door, down the hallway and into the kitchen. He was about to go *POP*, but he chomped over to the overflowing porridge pan, bite by bite, and tapped a spoon on the side.

"*Stop, little pan, stop,*" he groaned. The pan immediately stopped cooking.

Meanwhile, in the high street, Dad woke up on the sofa. Something wasn't right … He looked around, and saw a lot of confused people, and *LOTS* of porridge. Cars were covered in it, pets were stuck fast in it, and shops couldn't open their doors because of it. Then he heard a familiar voice.

"The only way to clear our town of the porridge is to eat it," shouted the boy. He had shimmied up a lamp post so everyone could see him. "It's tasty and it's good for you too!"

So the owner of the local café handed round spoons and all the people in the town began to eat the porridge. Mouthful by delicious mouthful, the flood went down, until Dad and his sofa were back on dry land.

The little boy climbed back up his lamp post. He'd had an excellent idea.

"No one in this town should ever go hungry again," he called. "From now on, the magic porridge pan will be for everyone."

Everyone was too busy cheering to notice the old woman at the back of the crowd who smiled as she turned and trundled away, pulling her shopping trolley behind her.

BANANA AND POPPY SEED PORRIDGE

Makes 3 small bowls

Ingredients

160g rolled porridge oats

pinch of salt

600ml whole milk

1 tsp ground cinnamon

2 bananas, peeled and sliced

30g flaked almonds

poppy seeds, for sprinkling

honey, for drizzling

Method

🍌 Place the oats, salt and milk in a medium pan and cook over a high heat, stirring continuously, until the porridge thickens.

🍌 Add the cinnamon and stir through.

🍌 Serve in bowls, topped with sliced banana and flaked almonds, a sprinkling of poppy seeds and a drizzle of honey.

Nadiya's tip

You could top your porridge with berries or sunflower seeds. Have fun trying lots of different combinations!

Kindness and
CUSTARD

There was a young boy who lived in a
quiet cul-de-sac in the corner of a sleepy town. Every night, he
walked home alone from school. It was only a short walk – just
three hundred metres – but the boy always dragged his feet and
took his time. His mum and dad worked long hours for very little
money, and he didn't often have very much to come home to.

Today, the boy had tried everything he could to slow down his
arrival home. He'd tickled a cat's tummy, watched a bumblebee
buzz around every blossom on a bush and avoided every crack
on the pavement, but he found himself at his front gate already.
The boy stepped up the path, oh so slowly, then pulled out the
key that was tied around his neck under his school uniform. He
opened the door to an empty house.

Heading to the kitchen, he spotted that his mum had left him
a small chunk of bread and a tiny sliver of cheese. This is what
he had every night for dinner. The boy quickly wolfed down his
meagre supper and ran upstairs to get changed.

Then he grabbed his coat and dashed to the newsagent to
start his evening job collecting payment from all the local houses

for their daily newspaper delivery.

The boy's evening ticked by as he knocked on doors and waited for the payment. As he passed the local chip shop, his tummy grumbled. He rootled around in his pocket, but all he found was one used cotton bud, a rubber band and a green Lego brick. No money, as usual, so no snack.

He plodded along to the next door. *KNOCK KNOCK KNOCK!* Nothing. He tried again. This time a lady with her hair tied high in a top-knot opened the door. She had a baby in her arms, a muslin over her shoulder and she looked tired out.

"Oh, hello, I wasn't expecting you until later. Hang on, let me get my purse ..." she said, and thrust the baby at the boy to hold.

The boy wasn't sure what he should do with the baby, so he stuck out his tongue and pulled a funny face. The baby gurgled and chuckled, and the boy noticed with surprise that he had one brown eye and one green eye. Before he could make the child laugh again, the lady had returned to the door and scooped the baby back into her arms.

"*He likes you*," she said, smiling at the baby's happy face.

Then the boy noticed the most delicious smell wafting from the house. It was sweet and light and creamy, all at the same time. The poor boy's tummy made the most almighty rumbling sound and he flushed purple from his eyebrows to his toes.

The lady peered at him. "*Are you hungry?*" she asked. He nodded, too embarrassed to speak. So the lady bundled the boy into her kitchen and sat him down at the table, opposite the baby in his high chair.

Then she turned and busied herself at the oven. The boy licked his lips and rubbed his tummy and the baby giggled some more.

The scent filling the kitchen was so delicious it was almost unbearable. The boy closed his eyes, breathing in the sweet smells, and when he opened them again, there was a small china pot filled with something pale yellow and wobbly on the table in front of him.

"Freshly baked vanilla custard," the lady told him. "Straight from the oven, and now, straight into that tummy of yours. It sounds like it needs feeding!"

The boy gobbled up the creamy baked custard, and two more pots of it after that. Then, with another funny face for the baby with the brown and green eyes and a hug of thanks for his mother, the boy went on his way, full, happy, and determined to finish his work before it got dark.

Years went by and the boy grew into a young man. He never forgot the kindness of the lady who had fed him when he was hungry and decided that he wanted to show kindness to others in his own life. So he worked and studied hard, becoming a doctor. And, after many more years passed, he saved enough money to start his very own clinic. So the doctor returned home to the sleepy town where he grew up and built his clinic there.

One summer's day, a frail old lady shuffled into the doctor's clinic, helped by a man wearing sunglasses. The doctor welcomed the old lady into his treatment room and listened to her with gentleness and patience. When the appointment was finished, he escorted her back to her son in the waiting room.

The doctor gasped.

The lady's son had taken off his sunglasses and was smiling gratefully at the doctor. The man had one brown eye and one green eye.

The doctor prepared the old lady's bill himself, and handed her the envelope with a huge smile as she left. The old lady took it nervously – she didn't have a lot of spare money and doctor's bills could be expensive.

When she and her son were back in their car, she opened the envelope and pulled out the folded sheet of paper that was inside. Her eyes filled with tears. It wasn't a bill, it was a handwritten note from the doctor himself.

You paid for your treatment all those years ago, with the vanilla baked custard.

VANILLA BAKED CUSTARD

Makes 6

Ingredients

600ml double cream or whole milk

1 tsp vanilla bean paste

50g caster sugar

6 large egg yolks

Nadiya's tip

If you don't have vanilla bean paste at home, you can use vanilla extract instead.

Method

* Preheat the oven to 150°C fan/gas mark 3.

* Pour the cream or milk into a saucepan and add the vanilla bean paste. Heat until it just starts to boil, then take the pan off the heat.

* Mix the sugar with the egg yolks in a bowl until they are well combined.

* Slowly pour the hot cream or milk into the bowl, stirring continuously, then pour the mixture into 6 ramekins.

* Put the ramekins in a large roasting tray, and half-fill the roasting tray with hot water, so the water comes halfway up the edges of the ramekins.

* Place the tray in the oven and bake for 30–40 minutes, or until the custard is set, but still has a slight wobble in the centre. Remove from the oven.

* Remove the ramekins from the water and transfer to the fridge to chill for 1 hour before eating. Or, if you can't wait that long, eat them while they are still warm. The custard will be a bit runny, but will still taste delicious.

Hansel and Gretel and the
HOUSE OF TREATS

Hansel and Gretel

were twins who lived with their father and mother in a little flat. Their father was a carpenter but he didn't make very much money. These days, people could buy flat-packed furniture that they could build for themselves and nobody wanted anything made by carpenters any more. The family made do as best they could, but sometimes they didn't have very much to eat at home.

One day, Hansel and Gretel decided that they needed to do something to help. Without telling their parents, they went to the local newsagent's to ask for a job. But the newsagent didn't need new paperboys or papergirls. Hansel tried the garden centre, but they didn't need new people to water the plants. Gretel asked at the fast food joint, but they didn't need new people to flip burgers.

The twins were still determined to earn some money, so they decided to try and find a job in a different town. They hopped on their rusty old bikes and cycled off.

Hansel and Gretel had never cycled anywhere outside of their own town before, but they were clever children so they came up with a plan to make sure they didn't get lost.

They decided to remember things that they came across on their journey. First, they turned left at some traffic cones, then they circled around a barrier, passed some digger trucks and finally, ducked through some scaffolding. Hansel called out what he saw to Gretel, and Gretel repeated it back to him, so that between them they would remember every detail and be able to find their way home again.

But when the twins reached the next town, they still had no luck finding a job. They tried every shop and restaurant, but there were

no vacancies. The sad pair climbed back on their bikes and started to cycle home, but before long they noticed that they couldn't see any scaffolding, or any diggers, or any barriers or cones. Hansel suddenly realised that they had been cycling through roadworks and the workmen must have packed everything away while they had been in the town.

By now it was getting dark and Hansel and Gretel were completely lost. They were about to panic, when they turned a corner and there, in front of them, was a beautiful house, lit up in bright jewel colours. They knew they should never talk to strangers, but they were lost and hungry, and there was no one else around to help them.

They nervously knocked on the door. A little old lady opened it, just a tiny crack. The twins politely asked her where they were and whether they could call their parents to let them know they were safe.

The old lady beamed at the children and threw the door wide, welcoming them inside.

As they walked into the house, Hansel and Gretel could not believe their eyes. Everything in the house was made of treats! Their tummies started to rumble in delight. There was a chandelier made from *midget gems*, a sofa made from *marshmallows*, a *shortbread* footstool and a *lollipop* coat stand. Instead of glass in the windows, there was melted *boiled sweets*, and *caramel* gushed from *toffee* taps. There were *liquorice* dinner plates, stairs built out of *cola cubes* and curtains made from *candyfloss*.

The children blinked in astonishment as they looked around. The old lady told them to help themselves, and Hansel and Gretel started nibbling on a *cookie mallow cushion*. It was the best biscuit they had ever tasted.

But the old lady wasn't happy in her house of treats, as it got sticky when everything melted in the summer, and the only people who ever came to visit her were people who wanted to eat her furniture. All she wanted was not to be lonely any more and to find a carpenter to make her some proper furniture. But, she told the children, there just weren't any good carpenters any more, not now that you could buy flat-packed furniture.

The children put down their half-eaten cookie mallow cushions. They liked the old lady and didn't want to think about her being unhappy. So when they called their dad, they told him everything.

An hour later, Dad arrived, carrying his carpenter's toolbox. The old lady's face lit up at the sight of him, and she hurried Dad into her house, chattering about chairs and wardrobes and bookshelves.

Hansel and Gretel looked at each other and smiled.

From that day forward, the old lady kept Hansel and Gretel's dad busy with carpentry, paying him well for his work. She also found four new friends, as she went to the twins' house every Sunday for lunch, always bringing freshly baked cookie mallows with her.

COOKIE MALLOWS

Makes 7

Ingredients

200g unsalted butter, softened

125g soft brown sugar

100g caster sugar

2 medium eggs, beaten

1 tsp vanilla extract

275g plain flour

½ tsp bicarbonate of soda

¼ tsp baking powder

pinch of salt

200g dark chocolate chips

100g roasted hazelnuts, finely chopped

200g marshmallows

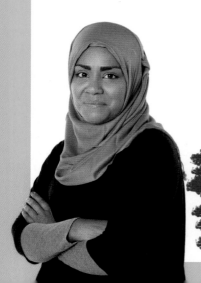

Nadiya's tip
You could use white and pink marshmallows to make different coloured cookie mallows.

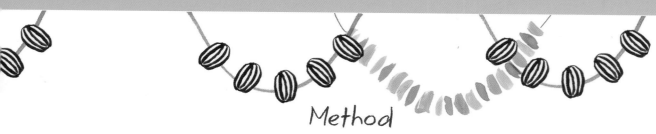

Method

- Preheat the oven to 180°C fan/gas mark 6. Line two baking sheets with greaseproof paper.

- Cream the butter and sugars together in a mixing bowl with an electric handheld whisk or in a stand mixer until light and fluffy, then add the beaten egg, a little at a time, scraping down the sides of the bowl to incorporate all the mixture. Stir in the vanilla extract.

- Sift the flour, bicarbonate of soda and baking powder into the bowl, then add the salt. Fold together, then add the chocolate chips and chopped hazelnuts and combine to make a dough.

- Using a tablespoon, place little mounds of dough on the lined sheets, leaving 5cm between each mound as they will spread.

- Transfer to the oven and bake for 12 minutes, or until light brown around the edges, then remove from the oven. Leave the cookies to cool on the baking sheets for 10 minutes then transfer to a wire rack.

- Melt the marshmallows in a bowl in the microwave in 1-minute bursts.

- Dollop a large mound of melted marshmallow on the underside of a cookie. Place another cookie on top and leave the filling to cool before eating.

68

The Billy Goats and the
CHEESE AND ONION TART

There were once three billy goat brothers

called Gruff. They had clip-cloppy hooves, beautifully groomed beards and were a bit of a whizz in the kitchen.

The Billy Goats Gruff had been forced to find a new meadow to graze in, as their local meadow had run out of clover. They were lazing about, having a chew on the nearby plants, when the littlest billy goat suddenly remembered something.

"We were going to make a tart today!" he exclaimed.

"Oh yes, little brother," said the middle billy goat, lazily. "Why don't you go and make a start, and we'll follow you ..."

The littlest billy goat was so keen to get baking that he scampered straight from the meadow to the shops to buy pastry. Then he scampered home by the quickest route he knew – the old stone bridge over the river. But in his excitement, the little goat had forgotten that a

stinky, warty troll lived underneath the bridge. A stinky, warty troll who was ALWAYS hungry.

TRIP, TRAP! TRIP, TRAP! went the little billy goat's hooves.

The noise woke up the troll.

"RARRRR! I smell pastry! Hand it over, my little goaty friend," the troll roared.

"Oh no," said little Billy Goat Gruff. "You don't want to eat that. The pastry's not even cooked. Eat my brother's ingredients. His are always tastier."

So the troll let the billy goat and his pastry pass.

Back at the meadow, the middle billy goat had eaten enough clover. "Shall we go and help with the tart?" he asked his big brother.

"In a minute," the biggest billy goat replied. "I'm still eating. Why don't you go now and I will follow you."

So the second billy goat bought some onions and then took the quickest way home. He'd also forgotten all about the troll.

TRIP, TRAP! TRIP, TRAP! went the middle billy goat's hooves.

"Aha!" growled the troll. "I've been expecting you, billy goat number two! Hand over your food, or else I'll have to eat you instead."

71

"I wouldn't if I were you," said middle Billy Goat Gruff. "My onions are raw. They will make your eyes water and make your breath even worse than it is already. My brother's on his way. His ingredients are always the best."

The troll let him pass, and went to clean his teeth.

Meanwhile, the eldest billy goat brother had finished his clover. He heaved himself to his hooves and clip-clopped his way to the shops, where he bought cheese. This billy goat was as forgetful as his younger brothers, and took the old stone bridge home.

TRIP, TRAP! TRIP, TRAP! went the eldest billy goat's hooves. The troll jumped up, his clean teeth gleaming.

"Mmmmm! Cheeeeeeeeeese!" cackled the troll. "Got any crackers to go with that?"

"No, I do not!" replied big Billy Goat Gruff. "And you should be ashamed of yourself, Mr Troll, picking on a poor little billy goat!"

The troll's warty face fell and he started to cry. "I—I ... I just wanted to try your cooking ... the Billy Goats Gruff's food is famous throughout the land!"

Being the big brother, the eldest goat was very bossy, but he also had a huge heart. "Well, that is very nice of you to say so, Mr Troll," he said, "but rather than frightening us and trying to steal our ingredients, wouldn't it be better if you just asked us nicely?"

The troll looked confused.

"If you promise to be on your best behaviour, you can come back to our house with me and try our cooking," said the billy goat kindly.

The troll couldn't have been happier. His new friends, the Billy Goats Gruff, taught him to cook, and he opened his own restaurant at the end of the old stone bridge. And the special dish at the Trip Trap restaurant? Why, goat's cheese and onion tart, of course!

GOAT'S CHEESE AND CARAMELISED ONION TART

Makes 6 slices

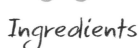

Ingredients

450g puff pastry

2 tbsp olive oil

1 large red onion, thinly sliced

3 tbsp balsamic vinegar

1 tsp soft brown sugar

150g goat's cheese, diced

salt and black pepper

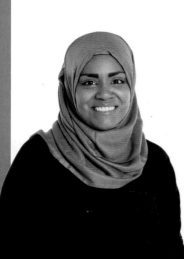

Nadiya's tip

The tart is delicious served hot or cold.
You could serve it cold with salad or hot
with some steamed vegetables. Yum!

Method

 Preheat the oven to 200°C fan/gas mark 7. Line a baking tray with greaseproof paper.

 Roll out the pastry to a rectangle measuring approximately 25x30cm, then transfer the pastry to the lined baking tray. Prick the pastry all over with a fork.

 Heat the oil in a frying pan, then add the onion, vinegar, sugar and a sprinkling of salt and pepper. Cook over a medium heat, stirring frequently, for 10 minutes, until the onions have softened and browned slightly. Spread the caramelised onion evenly over the pastry.

 Scatter the diced goat's cheese over the onion, then bake the tart in the oven for about 30 minutes, until the edges of the pastry are golden brown. Remove from the oven and serve warm, or leave to cool.

Rapunzel's Enchanted
CARROTS

One day a man and his wife were walking in the

woods a few miles from home. They were happy because they were about to have a baby, but it was also a sad day as the man had just lost his job. He was an optician, yet all of a sudden, no one in the village seemed to need glasses any more.

The man suspected it had something to do with the rumour about an old lady in the woods who grew and sold the most stupendous carrots. They were said to be the largest, crispest and brightest-orange carrots that anyone had ever seen. Some even said they were enchanted. And everyone knew that eating carrots helped your eyesight.

As the man and woman wove their way through the trees trying to cheer each other up, they came across a tiny cottage.

"That's odd," said the woman. "I've never seen that cottage before, and I walk in the woods all the time."

They peered over the gate and gasped at the sight of a huge vegetable garden bursting with life. There were cabbages, courgettes, green beans, and row upon row upon row of carrots.

"Let's have a closer look," the man whispered.

There didn't seem to be anyone around, so he took his wife's hand and they crept through the gate. The man kneeled down and pulled the leafiest carrot out of the ground. It was so orange it could have glowed in the dark, and it looked mouthwateringly juicy.

The man offered the carrot to his wife. She took a bite, and the CRUNCH echoed through the garden. Before they knew it, they had crunched and munched their way through all the carrots in the vegetable patch. They curled up for a nap in the cabbage patch, their tummies full.

The sound of a door slamming woke the snoozing man and woman with a start. A wrinkly, warty old lady was looming over them, wagging her bony finger and shouting.

"How dare you steal my carrots! You'll pay for this," she yelled.

The sorry pair were very embarrassed and promised to pay the old lady back as soon as the man got a new job, but she just turned and stomped away, muttering under her breath.

A few months later, the man and his wife had a beautiful baby girl they called Rapunzel. She was the light of their life. The man found another job and went back to the woods

with money to repay the old lady for the carrots. But he couldn't find her. The cottage had completely disappeared.

Everything was happy again for the man and his wife, until one morning, when they found their daughter's bed empty. They were distraught. It was all over the news, and everyone in the country was searching far and wide for the little girl. But it was no surprise that no one could find her, for the old lady from the cottage, who was really a witch, had snatched her and imprisoned her in a high tower block.

Rapunzel's room in the tower block only had one window and one door, but it had a little kitchen that she loved to use. The witch would visit every morning, bringing carrots with her, so Rapunzel got really good at carrot recipes. She also had a karaoke machine and a chest stuffed full of thousands of pairs of glasses, so she baked, and sang karaoke, and examined the glasses, day after day. She found glasses completely fascinating, but she couldn't work out why.

By now, Rapunzel's hair had grown really long, so the old witch would call up to the window, "*Rapunzel, Rapunzel, let down your hair.*"

Rapunzel would gather up her hair, which she'd plaited into a hefty rope, then she would throw it out of the window and wait for the witch to climb up.

This was the only life poor Rapunzel knew.

One day, a young man came riding past the tower block on his shiny green BMX. The sound of Rapunzel singing karaoke was so beautiful, it nearly made him fall off his bike.

The boy hid behind a nearby holly bush and looked up at the window. The singing girl was as lovely as her voice, and he fell head over heels for her in a heartbeat. He could not believe his eyes when an old warty lady came along, called to the girl and climbed up her long hair.

The boy was a bit shy. He came back day after day, but he could never pluck up the courage to do anything about his love for Rapunzel. But one day, her singing was just so unbearably lovely, he ran to the bottom of the block, copied what he'd heard the witch calling, and climbed up the plaited hair that dropped down to him. Rapunzel couldn't believe her eyes when a boy with a friendly smile tumbled through her window instead of the witch.

They ate carrot cake and talked for hours about all the things Rapunzel hadn't done, like ride a bike, or go to the cinema, or ice-skate. When the boy climbed back down her plait, he promised Rapunzel he would save her and teach her how to ride his BMX.

The next day, the old lady snagged Rapunzel's hair as she climbed.

"Ow! The boy didn't pull on my hair when he climbed up it yesterday! Maybe you should start using the lifts," Rapunzel blurted out, before she realised what she had said.

The witch was very angry that someone else had been in the room and chopped off Rapunzel's lovely hair with the bluntest fish knife in the kitchen.

The boy arrived that afternoon, shoved his BMX under the holly bush and called up to Rapunzel. The plait tumbled down and the boy climbed up it, but, to his horror, the witch was waiting at the top. She pushed him from the tower, and he fell headfirst into the holly bush, pricking his eyes on the spiky leaves. He could barely see.

Rapunzel looked out of the window at the boy she loved, staggering about with his hands over his eyes and something snapped inside her. She grabbed the plait and used it to tie the witch to a chair. Then she grabbed a freshly baked batch of carrot

cookies, wrapped up as many pairs of glasses as she could in a bed sheet and left the tower and the witch behind forever, singing with joy as she went.

Down on the ground, the boy could hear her song, but couldn't believe it when the sound got closer … and closer … until it was right in his ear. He couldn't see very well, but he knew it was his Rapunzel.

She spread out the bed sheet on the floor, guided the boy to sit down, and fed him a cookie to make him feel better. Then, she rootled through all the glasses until she found the perfect pair. She slid them on to the boy's nose and he gasped – he could see again!

They spent the whole afternoon eating carrot cookies, doing wheelies on the BMX and making plans for the future.

"What do you want to be when you're older, Rapunzel?" the boy asked.

"An optician," she replied. "It just feels like it's who I am."

CARROT AND NUTMEG COOKIES

Makes 6

Ingredients

1 small carrot, grated

100g rolled porridge oats

90g plain flour

1½ tsp baking powder

1½ tsp ground nutmeg

pinch of salt

30g unsalted butter, softened

1 large egg

1 tsp vanilla extract

120g runny honey

Method

- Preheat the oven to 180°C fan/gas mark 6. Line a baking tray with greaseproof paper.

- Mix the grated carrot in a bowl with the oats, flour, baking powder, nutmeg, salt, butter, egg, vanilla extract and honey, until well combined.

- Using a tablespoon, place dollops of the mixture on the lined baking tray, leaving 5cm between each mound as they will spread.

- Bake in the oven for 12–15 minutes, until golden around the edges and paler in the centre, then remove from the oven and transfer the cookies to a wire rack to cool.

Nadiya's tip

Breaking eggs into a bowl is great fun for kids of all ages – just try not to get any egg shell in the cookie mix!

The Littlest Dragon's
CINNAMON
BISCUITS

There were once two young dragons

who loved playing fancy dress. Their dressing-up box was full to bursting with all the costumes their mum had helped them make for playtime. They'd been pirates, bakers, astronauts, pop-stars and even mermaids.

One day, a big fancy dress competition was announced in the dragon caves. The little dragons scampered off to find their mum.

"Mum, can I be a robot? Please mum, pleasepleaseplease!" the older of the two young dragons begged.

"Mum, I really, really, REALLY want to be an elephant, with a trunk and big ears and EVERYTHING!" his little sister gasped, flapping her wings and puffing tiny smoke rings in excitement.

The little dragons' mum smiled at her children. "A robot and an elephant ... We should get to work right away then, shouldn't we?" she said.

So, while the older dragon went to visit grandpa, who had a huge hoard of silver and jewels in his cave, his little sister scurried off to see the wizard who lived next door.

Before long, the young dragons returned to show Mum what they had for their costumes.

Big brother dragon was carrying a cauldron full of liquid silver. "Grandpa breathed fire on some coins and melted them," he said. "We can dip loo rolls in the melted silver to make my robot costume!"

Little sister dragon had a long woolly sock. She looked worried.

"The wizard gave me one of his winter socks," she said. "I thought I could stuff it with moss from the walls of our cave to make my trunk. BUT, I can't think of anything for making my big elephant ears."

Mum racked her brains, but couldn't think of anything either.

The little dragon burst into tears. She so wanted to dress up as an elephant.

Suddenly, Dad appeared from the kitchen, carrying a baking tray.

Dragons love to bake, as they can use their fiery breath instead of an oven.

"DO I HEAR CRYING?" Dad boomed. "That won't do! As every dragon knows, the best cure for tears is biscuits."

He picked up two of his freshly baked cinnamon palmier biscuits from the tray, held them up to the side of his head and waggled them to make his daughter laugh.

The littlest dragon cheered up, and smiled at her dad. Then she gasped – she'd suddenly had a brilliant idea!

The day of the competition arrived, and the two young dragons got into their costumes and joined the fancy dress parade. There was a fairy and a firefighter and a clown and a witch, and many more.

The judges were very impressed by all the costumes, but it was an easy decision for them to make.

"The winner of the best fancy dress is ... robot dragon!" they announced.

The little dragon cheered her big brother as he went up to collect his award, but secretly, she was a bit sad not to win. But then, to everyone's surprise, the judges made another announcement.

"And now," they said, "we have a very special prize to award. The winner of the TASTIEST fancy dress is … elephant dragon, with her delicious cinnamon palmier biscuit ears!"

And the littlest dragon, with her woolly sock trunk and her dad's biscuits for ears, trotted up to collect her very special prize.

"From now on," she said, "these biscuits will be known as elephant ears!"

CINNAMON PALMIERS

Makes 12

Ingredients

450g puff pastry

1 egg, beaten

150g caster sugar

1½ tsp ground cinnamon

flour, for dusting

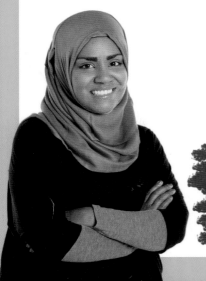

Nadiya's tip

Puff pastry is available ready-rolled,
if you need to make your biscuits quickly!

Method

🔥 Roll out the puff pastry to a rectangle about 4mm thick, then lightly brush the top of the pastry with the beaten egg.

🔥 Combine the sugar and cinnamon in a bowl. Sprinkle the mixture across the entire surface of the pastry.

🔥 With the short end of the rectangle facing you, roll both long ends in to the middle, so they meet at the centre.

🔥 Brush the rolled pastry with a little more of the beaten egg where the two rolls of pastry meet, then place the pastry on a baking tray and refrigerate for 30 minutes. Line a baking tray with greaseproof paper.

🔥 Cut the chilled pastry into 1.5cm-thick pieces, then gently roll out each piece on a floured surface to roughly 1cm thickness. Place the pieces on the lined baking tray. Chill in the fridge for a further 10 minutes and preheat the oven to 200°C fan/gas mark 7.

🔥 Brush each palmier with more egg and bake in the oven for 8–10 minutes, until golden brown.

Cinderella, the Party and the
PUMPKINS

Cinderella lived in a big house.

A never-ending, enormous house. It was a good job it was big, because Cinderella lived there with her gran, her great-auntie, her mum, her stepdad, her two stepsisters, two parrots, the cat and the pregnant dog.

Since she was a little girl, Cinderella had known that if she wanted something, she would have to go out and get it herself. So she went to college in the mornings, worked in a DIY shop in the afternoons and had an evening job cleaning plates in a restaurant.

The rest of Cinderella's family were very lazy, so when she got home there would always be more work to do – laundry, or washing up, or floors that needed mopping, or birdcages that needed cleaning out. When she eventually made it to bed, poor Cinders had to share it with the pregnant dog.

One night, as Cinderella lay curled up beside the dog, her stepsisters came in, waving their phones about. The town hall was throwing a massive Halloween party and EVERYONE was invited. Cinderella was so excited.

"When is it?" she asked her stepsisters.

"Friday," the stepsisters said, without looking up from their phones.

Cinderella thought for a while. Then she realised she was working an extra shift at the DIY shop on Friday evening. She quickly sent an email to her boss to ask for the time off, then tried to get back to sleep, but she couldn't stop thinking about the party. She tossed and turned. The pregnant dog was not impressed.

The next morning, Cinderella woke up to the sound of her sisters preparing for the party.

"There's only three days to go!" one sister shrieked.

Cinderella rolled her eyes, but she secretly wished she could join in with their pampering. Then she remembered she was waiting for an email from her boss at the DIY shop. She checked her messages and her heart sank into her boots.

'In response to your email, I cannot give you the night off because all other staff will be at the Town Hall Party. I need you at the shop to prepare for the massive screwdriver sale we're having on Saturday. It's going to be the biggest we've ever had!'

Cinderella would not be going to the party.

97

When Friday came, Cinders watched her stepsisters put on their beautiful dresses as she put on her itchy shop apron. She watched them slip their feet into their sparkly high heels as she laced up her steel-toecap boots. She watched them slick on their lipstick and primp their hair as she applied some lip balm and plonked her work cap on her head. Then they stepped into their pink limousine as Cinderella trudged off to the bus stop.

Once Cinderella got to work, she decided she needed to distract herself from thinking about the party. So she polished every screwdriver in the shop. Then she polished all the hammers. And all the spanners and all the wrenches. She even polished every single nut and bolt. When Cinders ran out of things to polish, she moved on to rearranging the pumpkins in the Halloween display.

The bell on the door rang as someone came into the shop. Not a single person had been in all evening, so Cinderella was startled by the sound. It was the boss's wife.

"How can I help?" Cinders asked, politely.

"No, my dear. The question should be — how can I help YOU?" the boss's wife replied with a kind smile. "I saw your email last night and I told my husband to give you the time off, but he'd already told all the other staff they could go to the party. No customers are going to come in while there's a party on, so I'm here to make sure you don't miss out on the fun."

Cinderella couldn't believe her ears.

"Now, Cinderella," the woman continued, "just think of me as your fairy godmother. I can't do magic but I can certainly work a miracle with party clothes ..." And she whipped out a silvery dress and a pair of jewel-encrusted shoes, hurrying Cinderella into the back to get changed.

When Cinders came out in the silver dress, the boss's wife clapped. "Oh, it looks so much better on you than it ever did on me," she said.

"Thank you for being so kind to me, but I can't leave the shop," Cinders said, sadly. "The boss will give me the sack."

"Oh don't worry about him," the woman said. "I'll take over until closing time. Just make sure you are back by then to close up, as I don't know the code to set the alarm."

Cinderella grinned, stuffed her uniform into her bag and ran out of the shop, before the boss's wife could change her mind.

Everyone stared as Cinderella walked into the party in her sparkly heels and shimmering dress. But Cinders was starving, so she ignored the staring and went straight to the buffet. She had spent so long on the Halloween display, she was longing for some pumpkin. She reached for the last pumpkin flapjack on the table … and bashed hands with a young man who was also reaching for the flapjack.

Cinderella looked up, and into a pair of kind dark-brown eyes.

"It's yours," the young man said. "But only in exchange for a dance."

She didn't argue. The pumpkin flapjack had given Cinders her energy back, and before long, she and the young man were shimmying on the dance floor. They danced the night away, until Cinderella remembered that she had to get back in time to close the shop, and the last bus left in three minutes!

She grabbed her bag and dashed off in such a rush she didn't have a chance to say anything to the young man. He was really sad, until he noticed she'd dropped something by the town hall door. It was Cinderella's work cap, and it had the name of a DIY shop on it …

The next afternoon, Cinderella was slumped at the counter in the shop. She was counting screwdrivers, but she was thinking about about silvery dresses and dancing, and the lovely young man whom she would never see again. She sighed – she'd felt so special, but now, it all just felt like a faraway dream.

TING-A-LING. The bell above the door tinkled. Cinderella was too sad to look up. Then a bag of flapjacks landed on the counter in front of her.

"They're yours," said the young man, as he gently put Cinderella's cap back on her head. "But only if you promise to dance with me always."

PUMPKIN AND SPICE FLAPJACKS

Makes 9 squares

Ingredients

100g golden syrup

100g soft light brown sugar

125g unsalted butter, softened

250g rolled porridge oats

75g pumpkin seeds

¼ tsp ground cinnamon

¼ tsp ground nutmeg

¼ tsp ground star anise

¼ tsp ground ginger

pinch of salt

(You will need a spice grinder for the star anise)

Nadiya's tip

Younger children might enjoy pressing the mix into the tin, while older children might like to measure out the spices.

Method

🎃 Preheat the oven to 180°C fan/gas mark 6. Line a 20cm square baking tin with greaseproof paper.

🎃 Combine the syrup, sugar, butter, oats, pumpkin seeds, spices and salt in a large bowl and mix until they all come together.

🎃 Press into the lined tin with the back of a spoon, then bake for 20–25 minutes, until golden brown all over.

🎃 Remove from the oven then turn out of the tin and leave to cool for 20 minutes.

🎃 Cut into squares once completely cooled.

The Pied Piper and the
STRIPIEST CAKE
IN TOWN

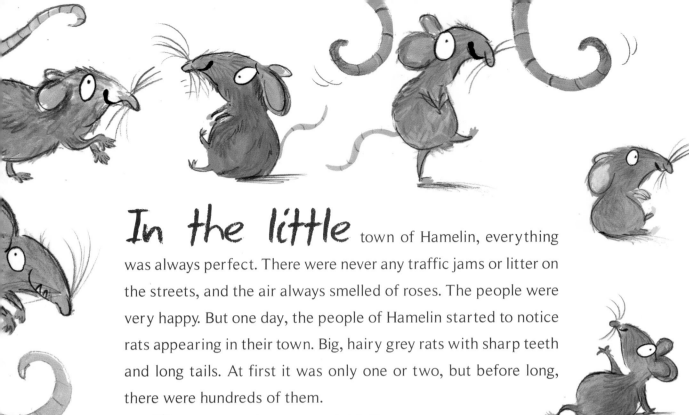

In the little town of Hamelin, everything

was always perfect. There were never any traffic jams or litter on the streets, and the air always smelled of roses. The people were very happy. But one day, the people of Hamelin started to notice rats appearing in their town. Big, hairy grey rats with sharp teeth and long tails. At first it was only one or two, but before long, there were hundreds of them.

"There are rats on my table!" said the postman.

"There are rats under my chair!" said the newsagent.

"There are rats in my kitchen!" said the childminder.

"There are rats in my bed!" said the lollipop lady.

"Someone make these rats go away!" begged a little girl.

So the people of Hamelin went to see their mayor. They pleaded with him to help, but the mayor said, "There are rats in my house, too. I can't get rid of them, so we shall all have to learn to live with them."

The townspeople were really unhappy, but there was nothing they could do.

One day a stranger in a stripy jumpsuit came to Hamelin. He went straight to see the mayor. "I am the Pied Piper, exterminator for the county," said the stranger. "I hear you have a rat problem?"

The mayor couldn't believe his luck. "I see you like stripes. If you can make these rats go away, I will reward you with the stripiest, yummiest cake you have ever tasted," he said.

"I can make them go away," said the Pied Piper. "And, as I don't know how to bake for myself, I would dearly love such a cake. The stripier the better, please."

They shook hands on their deal. The Pied Piper took a pipe from the pocket of his jumpsuit and began to play. He danced up Hamelin High Street, merrily blowing into the pipe, but no sound was coming out. The people were baffled – what was the stranger doing? Then, the hundreds of rats that were lining the pavements suddenly stopped in their tracks, pricked up their ears, and started following the piper up the street.

The Pied Piper headed towards the river, still playing the soundless tune on his pipe. One by one, the rats jumped into the water and swam away. Hamelin was rat-free once more!

The Pied Piper went back to the mayor's office to collect his reward, but no one answered the door when he knocked. The piper knew the mayor was inside. "The rats have all gone," he called through the letterbox. "Please give me the stripy cake you promised me, as I have done what you asked."

"Oh. Ah. Er. No ... Sorry," came the muffled voice of the mayor through his office door. "I'm too busy doing important mayor-type stuff to worry about baking you a cake."

"Very well," said the Pied Piper, "I will play a different tune, and then you'll wish you hadn't been too busy to keep your side of the deal."

So the piper went out into the streets and began to play another tune without any sound. The people looked around them – there weren't any rats left, so why was the piper still playing?

Then came a rumbling sound from far away. It grew louder, and louder, and LOUDER. Suddenly, a wall of grey appeared on the horizon. The townspeople couldn't work out what it was, until the wall of grey reached the gates of Hamelin. It was thousands and thousands of rats, even more than there were before.

"Sorry everyone," the Pied Piper yelled over the stampede of rats. "The mayor broke his promise to give me a stripy cake, so I am leaving Hamelin and I'm taking my rat-catching secret with me."

The poor townspeople had no choice but to put up with the rats. They found the rodents everywhere – gnawing on their freshly baked bread, scattering litter from their bins and using their slippers for sleeping bags.

One day it got all too much for one old lady, so she gathered some of her friends from the Hamelin baking club.

"If it's a cake the Pied Piper wants, let's give him the most colourful, most delicious, STRIPIEST cake he has ever seen," she said. "Then he might forget that the mayor broke his promise."

So the baking club came up with a recipe that included all their favourite ingredients and created the most beautiful cake any of them had ever baked.

The Pied Piper was fishing on a riverbank just outside of Hamelin, when he was surprised to see a troupe of little old ladies staggering towards him, weighed down by a massive cake.

"Mr Pied Piper," they chorused, "we have baked you the stripy cake that you are owed. We are sorry the mayor broke his promise, but we hope you will help the people get their town back."

The Pied Piper was moved to tears by the beauty and the taste of the old ladies' cake. After one bite, he put down his fishing rod, returned to town and piped the rats away.

The very next day, the town's people held an election. The Pied Piper was to be their new mayor. And the old mayor got a new job too … as Hamelin's Chief Litter Collector!

ZEBRA CAKE

Makes 1 cake

Ingredients

For the cake

175g unsalted butter, softened, plus
   extra for greasing

175g caster sugar

225g self-raising flour

1½ tsp baking powder

3 medium eggs

1 tsp almond extract

1½ tbsp cocoa powder

For the icing

25g unsalted butter

15g cocoa powder, sifted

2 tbsp milk

100g icing sugar

25g white chocolate

Method

♪ Preheat the oven to 180°C fan/gas mark 6. Lightly grease a 900g loaf tin, and line the base of the tin with a strip of baking parchment, letting it overhang at both ends so you can pull the cake out after it's baked.

♪ To make the cake mixture, put the butter, sugar, flour, baking powder and eggs in a bowl and beat until well combined. Transfer half the cake mixture to a separate bowl.

♪ Stir the almond extract into the mixture in one of the bowls.

♪ Mix the cocoa powder with 2 tablespoons of hot water to make a paste. Add this to the other bowl and mix thoroughly.

♪ Randomly spoon dollops of each mixture into the prepared tin until both mixtures are finished. Smooth the top to make it level.

♪ Bake in the oven for 50–60 minutes. The cake should spring back when touched. Remove from the oven and leave to cool in the tin for 10 minutes, then turn it out and leave it to cool completely on a wire rack.

♪ For the icing, melt the butter in a small pan, then add the cocoa butter. Stir and cook gently for 1 minute, then stir in the milk and icing sugar and take the pan off the heat. Leave the mixture to cool completely, then spread it over the top of the cake.

♪ Melt the white chocolate and dollop it on top of the icing. Run the tip of a skewer through the dollops to give the icing a ripple effect and leave to set.

Nadiya's tip
You can also use a skewer to test if a cake is baked properly. Stick it into the centre – if it comes out clean, the cake is ready.

The Princess and the
PEA RISOTTO

Once there was a prince who was

stubborn. Very very stubborn. When the prince got an idea in his head, he would NEVER let it go. Once, he decided that he would only wear clothes made from the silk of glow-worms. Another time, he insisted that he would only eat yellow food for a whole year. The king and queen were getting a bit fed up with their stubborn son.

"It's time for you to get married," the king told the prince one day.

"I will only marry a real princess," the prince announced.

But real princesses were in short supply in the kingdom, so the king called for all young ladies who wanted to meet the prince to come to the castle.

"Is she a real princess?" the prince asked about a girl with a lovely smile. "Um, well ... no," said the queen. "But she is very friendly."

Guest Quarters

But the prince didn't want friendly, he wanted a real princess.

"*Is she a real princess?*" asked the prince about a girl with a wonderful laugh.

"*Afraid not,*" said the king. "*But she is very jolly.*"

But the prince didn't want jolly, he wanted a real princess.

Then, a girl from the kingdom next door came to see the king to ask for his help with a pressing matter. The king decreed he would give the girl lodging while he considered her request, and she was shown to the guest quarters in the castle.

But the prince had caught sight of the girl and had fallen instantly in love.

"*Is she a real princess?*" the prince asked.

"*I don't know, my son,*" the king said. "*She's from another kingdom.*"

The prince was so in love, the queen knew she had to do something to help her son. She thought long and hard, and came up with a plan.

"*A real princess is delicate, and very sensitive. She'll be used to sleeping on the softest of beds ...*" thought the queen. "*I know what to do ...*"

117

So the queen went to the guest quarters and slipped a pea beneath the mattress on the girl's bed. Then she put another mattress on top, and another on top of that, and another. The queen crossed her fingers and her toes that the girl was a real princess, and would feel the lumpy pea underneath all the mattresses when she went to bed.

The next morning, the queen went to the girl's room.

"How did you sleep, my dear?" the queen asked.

"I had the best sleep of my life, your majesty," said the girl. "The bed was as smooth as silk with no wrinkles or bumps to keep me awake."

The queen's heart sank. The girl wasn't a real princess.

"And I had the most wonderful dream," the girl continued. "It was all about peas. And it gave me a brilliant idea. Will you take me to the kitchens please?"

"Please tell me, is she a real princess?" the prince begged his mother later.

"No, my son," said the queen, sadly. "But she is a remarkable chef and she is very clever indeed. I have appointed her Chief Cook at the palace, so I can have more of her delicious pea risotto. Try some!"

The prince was sad that the girl wasn't a princess and that he wasn't going to marry her, but he tasted the bowl of risotto that his mother offered him anyway.

The stubborn prince couldn't believe his tastebuds, and decided right there and then that he didn't need to marry a real princess after all. He wanted to marry this girl, who was lovely and clever and an amazing cook.

So the prince went to his vegetable patch. He was very proud of the herbs he grew there. He picked some mint and took it to the girl.

"I think this mint will be perfect with your delicious pea risotto," said the prince, blushing a little. "And ... will you marry me?"

"I will," said the girl. "And we can cook together for the rest of our days."

PEA AND MINT RISOTTO

Serves 4

Ingredients

50g salted butter

1 medium onion, finely chopped

300g frozen peas

350g risotto rice

1 tsp salt

200ml white grape juice

1.7 litres hot vegetable stock

25g Parmesan cheese, grated

2 handfuls of fresh mint leaves, chopped

olive oil, for drizzling

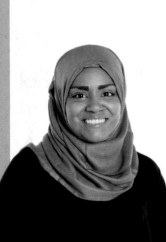

Nadiya's tip

If you don't have a food processor, defrost the peas then give them a good mash with a fork.

Method

- Melt the butter in a wide pan over a medium heat, then turn down the heat to low, add the onion and cook for about 10 minutes. Stir frequently, until the onions are really soft but not browned.

- While the onions are cooking, place half the frozen peas in the bowl of a food processor with a splash of water and blitz until smooth.

- Add the rice and salt to the onion, increase the heat to high and toast the rice in the butter for 1 minute, then pour in the grape juice and stir until the liquid is completely absorbed.

- Reduce the heat to medium and add the hot stock a ladleful at a time, stirring between each addition until the liquid is absorbed.

- Repeat the process until the stock is finished. This can take up to 30 minutes.

- Stir in the puréed peas, the remaining whole peas and the Parmesan, reduce the heat to low and cook, stirring, for a further 10 minutes, until the whole peas are cooked.

- Serve sprinkled with fresh mint and drizzled with lashings of olive oil.

Snow White and the
APPLE

There was once a girl with hair the

colour of midnight and skin the colour of pearls. Her parents called her Snow White. Soon after the little girl started school, her parents decided to live in separate houses. But even though they lived in different places, they still loved their Snow White more than anything else in the world. She would stay with her dad in his beautiful house in the country during school holidays, where she loved nothing better than to sit underneath the apple tree in the garden, eating its ruby-red apples, reading and daydreaming. It was where Snow White felt true happiness.

Years passed and Snow White's dad married again. Snow White's stepmum was beautiful, but she was also very vain and would admire herself in the mirror for hours every day. She didn't like it when Snow White came to stay, for Snow White was not only beautiful, she was kind and caring, and everyone loved her. Her stepmum was jealous and was often unkind to Snow White.

One summer, Snow White's stepmum said she couldn't come to stay and she would never be welcome there again.

Snow White's dad was very sad about it. "I need to talk to your stepmum," he told his daughter on the phone. "I will make this better. I promise."

Snow White was very sad too, but at least she had university to look forward to. She'd found a lovely house to move into, and seven new friends to live with.

All of her flatmates were different. Her first friend had allergies and sneezed a lot. Her second friend worked night shifts at the supermarket, so he was always tired. Her third friend had a lovely smile and always looked on the bright side of life. Her fourth friend was really clever and training to be a doctor. Her fifth friend was sensitive and often got cross when the others didn't do the washing-up or forgot to put the bins out. Her sixth friend had a heart of gold but was always daydreaming. And the seventh friend was quiet and shy and spent most of his time in his room.

Snow White loved him best of all, as they would talk for hours and hours when no one else was around.

Snow White's friends knew all about her dad and her stepmum, and how much Snow White longed to sit in the shade of the apple tree again. They all looked after Snow White when she got sad about it, bringing her cups of tea and giving her cuddles.

One day, Snow White was staring out of her bedroom window when she saw someone familiar walking up the path towards the house. Her heart pounded in her chest. Then there was a sharp rapping at the front door.

Snow White went to the door, took a deep breath and opened it.

"*Hello,*" she said to the person standing there on the doorstep.

"*Hello, Snow White,*" said her stepmum. "*May I come in?*"

Snow White let her stepmum into the house and led her to the kitchen. Her stepmum held out a lumpy bag. "*For you,*" she said.

Snow White peered inside, and saw it was full of ruby-red apples. She blinked away a tear.

"I came to say sorry," her stepmum continued. "Your dad is so sad, and it is all my fault. I brought you these apples because I know how much you love the tree at our house, so, please come and stay with us again. I'll make you my famous apple tart!"

Snow White plucked an apple from the bag and took a huge bite. But the bite was so big that, as she swallowed, the apple stuck in her throat and she began to choke.

Her stepmum panicked and screamed for help. But no one came. Flatmate one was out getting his allergy medicine. The second was fast asleep with earplugs in. The third was out at cheerleading practice, and the fourth was at the library. The fifth flatmate had gone off in a huff after breakfast, because flatmate six had forgotten to wash his cereal bowl, AGAIN. Number six had run after her to apologise.

By now, Snow White couldn't breathe. She was seeing stars and about to faint when flatmate seven came pelting into the kitchen. He grabbed her tightly around her chest and squeezed hard. The chunk of apple flew out of Snow White's mouth and she collapsed against her friend, gasping for air. He held her upright and stroked her hair as she choked and spluttered.

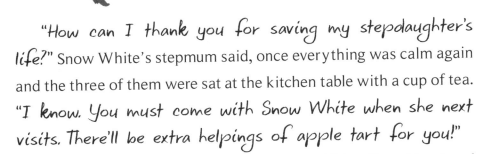

"How can I thank you for saving my stepdaughter's life?" Snow White's stepmum said, once everything was calm again and the three of them were sat at the kitchen table with a cup of tea. "I know. You must come with Snow White when she next visits. There'll be extra helpings of apple tart for you!"

The boy blushed and nodded, and Snow White slipped her hand into his under the table. It wouldn't be long before she could sit under her precious apple tree again. And what's more, she'd be taking a very special friend with her. Snow White was happy again.

FRENCH APPLE TART

Makes 1 tart

Ingredients

For the pastry

175g plain flour, plus extra
    for dusting
15g icing sugar
75g unsalted butter, plus extra
    for greasing
1 egg yolk

For the filling

50g unsalted butter
900g cooking apples, cored, peeled
    and cubed

2 tsp ground cinnamon
4 tbsp apricot jam
50g caster sugar
grated zest of 1 unwaxed lemon

For the topping

225g red apples
2 tbsp lemon juice
1 tsp caster sugar

For the glaze

4 tbsp apricot jam

Method

To make the pastry, put the flour, icing sugar and butter into a bowl. Rub the butter into the flour and sugar until the mixture resembles breadcrumbs. Add the egg yolk and 1 tablespoon of cold water, mix with a palette knife, then bring the dough together with your hands until you have a smooth ball. Wrap the dough in clingfilm and chill for 10 minutes in the freezer.

Preheat the oven to 200°C fan/gas mark 7. Lightly grease a 22cm round, fluted tart tin.

Dust the work surface lightly with flour and roll out the chilled pastry, then use it to line the base and sides of the tart tin, letting it hang over the edge as it will shrink during baking (you can trim the extra pastry away after it's cooked). Prick the pastry lightly with a fork, line the base with a circle of greaseproof paper and fill with baking beans.

Bake the pastry for 15 minutes, then take it out of the oven, remove the baking beans and greaseproof paper, and return to the oven for a further 5 minutes. Remove and set aside to cool.

For the filling, melt the butter in a large pan, then add the cooking apples and 2 tablespoons of water. Cover and cook for 15 minutes, until the apples are soft, then stir in the cinnamon, jam, sugar and lemon zest and cook until any remaining liquid has evaporated. Remove from the heat and leave to cool.

Once the filling is cool, spoon it into the pastry case.

Core and slice the red apples, and arrange them neatly on top of the tart. Brush with the lemon juice and sprinkle over the caster sugar.

Bake for 25 minutes, or until both the pastry and the apples are golden, then remove from the oven.

Warm the apricot jam in a pan and brush it all over the tart while it's still warm.

Nadiya's tip

Younger kids could rub the 'breadcrumbs' or sprinkle the caster sugar. Older kids could roll out the pastry or arrange the apple slices.

In a kingdom

not too far from here, a king and a queen had a healthy baby girl. The kingdom was filled with villagers and magical folk. Even the dragons came to see her. Everyone good was welcome.

"How precious she is!" the good fairies cried. They cast spells for the baby princess.

"Let her be kind," said one fairy, touching the baby's heart with her sparkling wand.

"Let her be clever," said another fairy, touching the baby's forehead.

But a bad fairy, who had not been invited, sneaked into the castle.

"Let her prick her finger and then her night will be everlasting!" the bad fairy cackled, touching the baby's fingertip before anyone could stop her.

The king and queen were terrified for their precious daughter, so they banned all sharp things from the kingdom. The people found it a bit tricky to sew on buttons or safety-pin things together, but they loved the princess so they didn't really mind.

As the years went by the princess grew into a very curious girl, with an imagination that never went to sleep. At night she would often go wandering in the castle in her slippers, exploring every nook and cranny.

One moonlit evening, she found a room in a tower that she'd never seen before. She picked the lock with a hair grip and went inside, but it was empty apart from one single window. The princess went to the window, put her hands on the windowsill and leaned out …

"*OW!*" she cried, looking down at her finger, where a little drop of blood was forming. The princess hadn't noticed the gnarled bush of thorns that had grown up the side of the tower, encircling the window frame. She rushed to her mother for a plaster, but didn't understand why the queen burst into tears at the sight of her finger. It was only a pinprick!

The king and queen waited in despair for the bad fairy's curse to come true and the princess to fall into a deep sleep forever. But that didn't happen. The princess was wide awake. All the time!

At first the princess was delighted – she could explore, and play, and have fun, all day, every day, without wasting time asleep. But after a whole week without sleep, the princess became frustrated and very grumpy. Her beautiful eyes were red and puffy and she walked around the castle in a daze, snapping at anyone who crossed her path. So the king and queen sent heralds out to the kingdom announcing that anyone who could help their daughter sleep would be rewarded with a lifetime's supply of safety pins.

First the princess was visited by a personal trainer. The trainer told the princess to get lots of exercise, and she would soon get to sleep. So the princess did five hundred squats, but all she got was an achy bottom.

Then the princess was visited by an air-conditioning specialist. The specialist told the princess to cool down her room and she would soon get to sleep. So the princess had an air-conditioning unit put into her bedroom, but all she got was the flu.

Next, the princess was visited by an author who wrote bedtime stories. The author told the princess she should read at night and she would soon get to sleep. So the princess read forty-five books, thrilling adventures about princes and princesses, dragons and trolls, but all she got was a racing heart.

Then she was visited by world-renowned baker Haul Pollywood, who travelled from the land of Wallasey. He brought her a box of marmalade cookies, with spices to make her sleepy. She ate a cookie. She chewed. Then she looked up at the baker with a steely gaze and said, *"they're tasty, but bake them a little longer next time."* The baker shuffled away. And the princess still couldn't sleep.

The princess had given up all hope of ever sleeping again, when there was a knock at her door. A tall, handsome young man dressed in chefs' whites walked in, carrying a wooden box. *"I am a chocolatier,"* he said, *"and in this box, I have the magic ingredients to send you to sleep."*

The princess sighed. She didn't think anything in this old wooden box could possibly hold anything magical, but she would turn cartwheels in her pyjamas if it meant she could just get to sleep!

The chocolatier opened the box and the most delicious smells wafted out.

"What is that?" the princess gasped. She had never smelled anything so wonderful in her life.

"It's magic," said the chocolatier.

He mixed all his ingredients together on the stove and poured a stream of steaming velvety liquid into a mug. He handed it to the princess and she breathed in the chocolatey vapour. She felt her pricked fingertip tingle and her body relax.

The chocolatier wrapped the princess in a snuggly blanket and held her tight as she drank. She lay her head on his shoulder and, as if by magic, the sleepless princess

finally

fell

asleep.

CARDAMOM AND MALT HOT CHOCOLATE

Makes 2 large mugs

Ingredients

2 tbsp cocoa powder

2 tbsp malt powder

2 tbsp runny honey

1 tsp ground cardamom

500ml whole milk

100ml single cream

small marshmallows

100g white chocolate, melted

Nadiya's tip

Why not get cosy, cuddle up with your hot chocolate and reread your favourite stories from the book?

Method

- Combine the cocoa, malt, honey and ground cardamom in a small saucepan. Add 6 tablespoons of water to the pan and mix everything together to form a paste.

- Place the pan over a low heat, letting it warm through gently, then add the milk and cream, increase the heat and bring to the boil, stirring continuously. As soon as the liquid bubbles, remove from the heat.

- Pour the hot chocolate into cups, top with marshmallows and drizzle with the melted white chocolate.

- Let the drink cool a bit before you enjoy it!

Thank you

To Musa, Dawud and Maryam. The loves of my life, my inspiration.

A massive thanks to my nephews Zayn, Deen and Adhiy, and my nieces Aleesha, Leeya, Maya and Leela for being an extension of my own children. Together, you guys make life louder, livelier and full of love.

To my husband Abdal. Every time I thought you weren't listening to my stories as I read them out, you would suddenly let out a giggle. Thanks for giggling!

To the mothers in my life: Nan, Mum, my sisters Jasmin, Sadiya and Yasmin, and my sister-in-law Lucy. Each day is different, each day is hard, but each day you guys rock and you do it with a smile on your face.

To my friend and agent Anne, for helping me through each and every day. You are the epitome of a hard-working mother and have shown me it can be done.

Thank you to the Hachette team: Emma, Alison, Fritha, Lucy, Lauren, Clare, Anne and Hilary, for believing in the idea and allowing it to take shape in its physical form. Without this team, *Bake Me a Story* wouldn't have come alive as it has. All those emails, late nights and meetings have meant I have a book that I am so very proud of.

Thanks also to Clair Rossiter for the incredible illustrations. Your artwork is simply stunning and really brings my stories to life.

To the grown-ups reading this book, I would like to dedicate this book to your inner child. Just when you think that kid inside you has gone, it rears its sweet, inquisitive head. Sometimes we have to remind ourselves that licking the bowls, flour fights and chocolate round the mouth is exactly who we still are.

And finally to all the kids — I hope you have had loads of fun reading the stories and trying the recipes. Keep baking and keep enjoying stories — you never know where your imagination might take you next!